RAID ON THE FORTH

The First German Air Raid on Great Britain in World War II

16 October 1939

HUGH HARKINS

RAID ON THE FORTH

THE FIRST GERMAN AIR RAID ON GREAT BRITAIN IN WORLD WAR II

16 OCTOBER 1939

Aviation Historical Research #2

© Hugh Harkins 2018

Centurion Publishing

United Kingdom

ISBN 10: 1-903630-73-8
ISBN 13: 978-1-903630-73-0

This volume first published in 2018

This research paper has adopted the Chicago Manual of Style referencing for bibliography and footnotes, although, in some instances, it forgoes shortened repeat notes or the use of *ibid* for the sake of clarity. It has, however, not always been possible to adopt a standard referencing format for much of the primary source documentation

CONTENTS

ABSTRACT   vii

1 AIR RAID ON THE FORTH – THE FIRST GENRMAN   9
   BOMBING RAID ON GREAT BRITIAN IN WORLD
   WAR II – 16 OCTOBER 1939

2 ADDENDUM I   39

3 ADDENDUM II   41

4 ADDENDUM III   43

5 BIBLIOGRAPHY   47

6 GLOSSARY   50

ABSTRACT

This research paper details the German air raid on British warships in the Firth of Forth on 16 October 1939 – the first German air raid on the United Kingdom during World War II. While this air raid has been documented over almost eight decades, in many areas fact gives way to non-fact. The paper utilises primary source documentation and, secondary source materials to separate that fact from non-fact. The paper details, in turn, the context surrounding the German air operation, the Operation itself and British operation to counter the air raid and details the material damage inflicted on the warships themselves. The paper also puts forward answers to a number of disputed questions, including the location of one of the ships that was bombed – the air raid actually targeting two separate points some 30 miles apart rather than a single raid on the anchorage off Rosyth as has ubiquitously gone down in history. The paper concludes with an assessment of the strategic aftermath of the raid, which was part of a concerted German campaign that had a profound effect on British defensive policy.

1

AIR RAID ON THE FORTH – THE FIRST GENRMAN BOMBING RAID ON GREAT BRITIAN IN WORLD WAR II – 16 OCTOBER 1939

On 16 October 1939, the German Luftwaffe launched an air raid on British warships located in the Firth of Forth Estuary on the East Coast of Scotland. This has been recorded as the first German air attack on Great Britain during World War II.[1] Through the use of archived primary source documentation, along with appropriate secondary source material, this research paper will address, in turn, the various aspects of the raid – the context of the raid, the German air reconnaissance and bomber force, the British defensive fighter operations, anti-aircraft defence, aircraft losses, damage inflicted to Royal Navy warships, air raid warning failure and the strategic aftermath.

The air raid is often discussed in isolation, but should be considered as part of a wider German assault on British warships in port, not only in the Firth of Forth, but also at the Royal Navy Home Fleet main anchorage at Scapa Flow in the Orkney Islands to the North of mainland Scotland. When taken as part of a concerted campaign, albeit small scale, then the first blow was struck against the Royal Sovereign (Revenge) class 15 inch gun Battleship HMS *Royal Oak*, which was torpedoed at anchor at Scapa Flow on the night of 14 October 1939 in an audacious attack by the Kriegsmarine submarine (U-Boat – Undersea Boat), U-47.[2] The submarine attack on Scapa Flow had taken place two days after Britain and France had rejected a German peace proposal. In this regard, it can be assumed that any earlier plans for attacking targets in British ports or anchorages had been held back pending the completion of the German

---

[1] The Luftwaffe was the German Air Force (Air Arm)

[2] The Kriegsmarine was the German Navy. U-Boat (Undersea Boat). U-47 was commanded by Lieutenant Gunther Prien

campaign in Poland.[3] Germany had hoped that the western allies, Britain and France, could be persuaded to accept the subjugation of Poland and make peace with Germany.

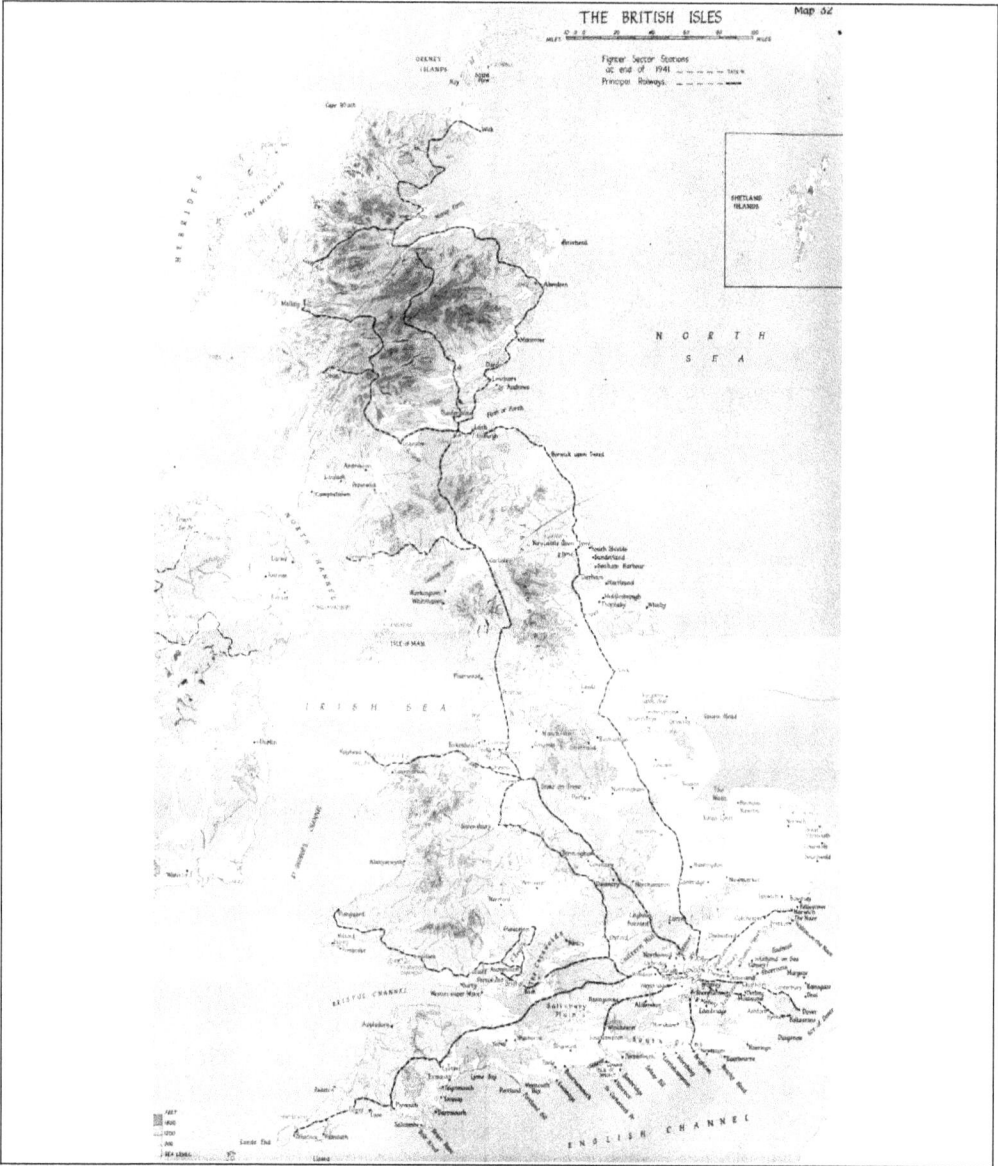

Figure 1. Map of the British Isles representative of 1939. CC

---

[3] The Soviet Union invaded Eastern Poland on 17 September 1939. Poland was effectively divided between Germany and the Soviet Union on the Polish capitulation

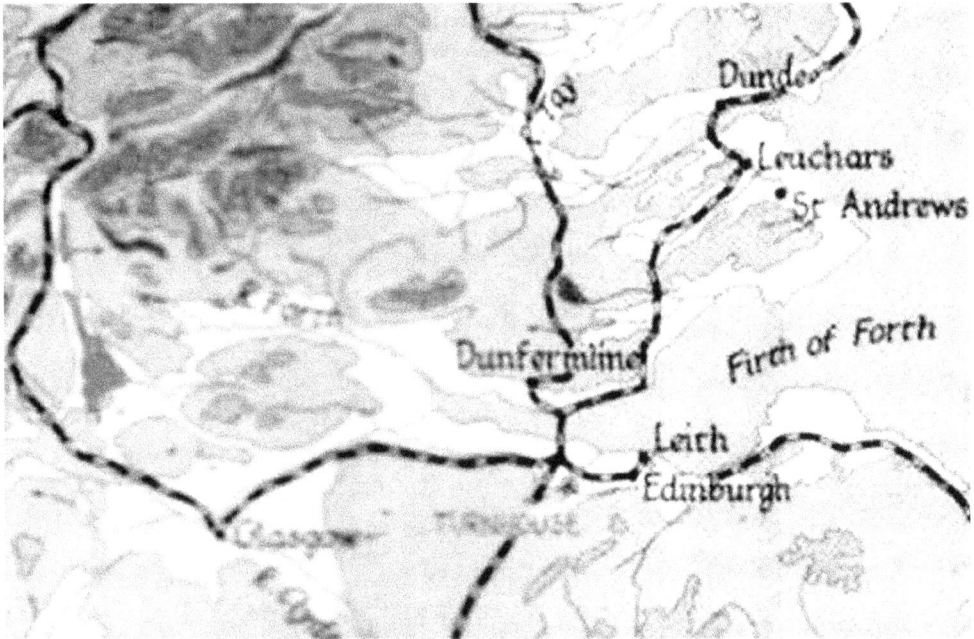

Figure 2. Close up section map of the Firth of Forth representative of 1939. CC

The early months of the war were still a time of relative civility in regards to air attacks between Germany and Britain. Each side, for their own reasons, wishing to avoid attacks on targets that could inflict civilian casualties. Since the outbreak of war on 3 September 1939, the RAF had flown a number of air raids by Vickers Wellington twin-engine heavy bombers and Bristol Blenheim twin-engine medium bombers against German warships in the areas of the Schillig Roads and the entrance to the Kiel canal on Germany's North Sea coast, with few claims of success and even less actual success.[4] The British aircrew were under orders to bomb only targets in the water and, at all costs, to avoid bombing shore targets. The German high command looked upon air attack as a way of taking the war to British shores, after a fashion, with a vastly reduced probability of inflicting civilian casualties and, at the same time, the reasonable likelihood of inflicting material damage to units of the British Home Fleet.

While it is no understatement to say that Great Britain was not prepared for war with Germany in 1939, it should be noted that while Germany was, to an extent, prepared for the possibility of a war in Western Europe, she was considerably less prepared for a maritime war with Britain in 1939. The Luftwaffe bomber fleets were primarily geared toward supporting German

---

[4] The Wellington would later be reclassified as a medium bomber and the Blenheim would be reclassified as a light bomber with the introduction of four engine heavy bombers. The town of Kiel lies on the German Baltic coast and the canal links it with Brunsbüttel on the North sea coast

Army ground offensives, a role in which it had proved very effective in the campaign in Poland in September 1939.[5] As summer 1939 had approached, the German Air Ministry laid the groundwork for the formation of a maritime strike force that would be tasked with attacking warships at anchor.[6] This led to a small Luftwaffe maritime strike force, which, by late summer 1939, consisted of *Kampfgeschwader 26* and *I/Kampfgeschwader 30*. The former was equipped with 65 Heinkel He.111 twin-engine medium bombers, of which 58 were declared operational, and the latter was equipped with twenty of the faster Junkers Ju.88 medium bombers, 13 of which were operational (these values were correct for 9 September 1939).[7]

The German attacks on Scapa Flow would resume on 17 October with an air raid against warships lying at anchor. However, first it would be the turn of the Firth of Forth, which, as noted above, was the subject of an air attack on the 16th of the month. It is probable that the German high command considered that any large warships returning to Scapa Flow following the submarine attack on the 14th would be directed to the anchorages off Rosyth – inviting targets for the pending air attack on the Firth of Forth. Such a view would be justified as in the immediate aftermath of the sinking of the *Royal Oak*, the Commander-in-Chief of the Home Fleet was ordered to facilitate the movement of the fleet to Rosyth by 21 October 1939.[8] On 16 October, it was expected that the Home Fleet would be based at Rosyth until the defences were strengthened at Scapa Flow (for example there was only one row of anti-submarine/torpedo nets, compared with three rows late in World War One), then estimated as 7 November 1939.[9]

---

[5] Organised resistance by the Polish Army effectively ended on the first day of October 1939 with the fall of the Hel Peninsula

[6] A.M. Pamphlet (Monograph) No.248, 96-97. See also Basil Collier, *History of the Second World War, The Defence of the United Kingdom*, United Kingdom Military Series (London, HMSO, 1957), 80

[7] A.M., A.H.B.-6 (Files of the Quartermaster General, German Air Ministry). See also Collier, *The Defence of the United Kingdom*, 80

[8] W.M. (39) 49th Conclusions, Minute 3. Confidential Annex. Naval Situation. Richmond Terrace, S.W.1, 16th October, 1939. See also Denis Richards, *History of the Second Word War, The Royal Air Force 1939-1945, Vol. I: The Fight At Odds*, United Kingdom Military Series, (London, HMSO, 1953), 66-67. Rosyth naval base/dockyard was situated on the North shore of the Forth Estuary less than 1 mile westward from the North end of the Forth Bridge. The Forth Bridge was situated around 5 km from the city of Edinburgh, with its South entrance several hundred metres to the East of the town of South Queensferry and its North entrance accessible from North Queensferry

[9] W.M. (39) 49th Conclusions, Minute 3

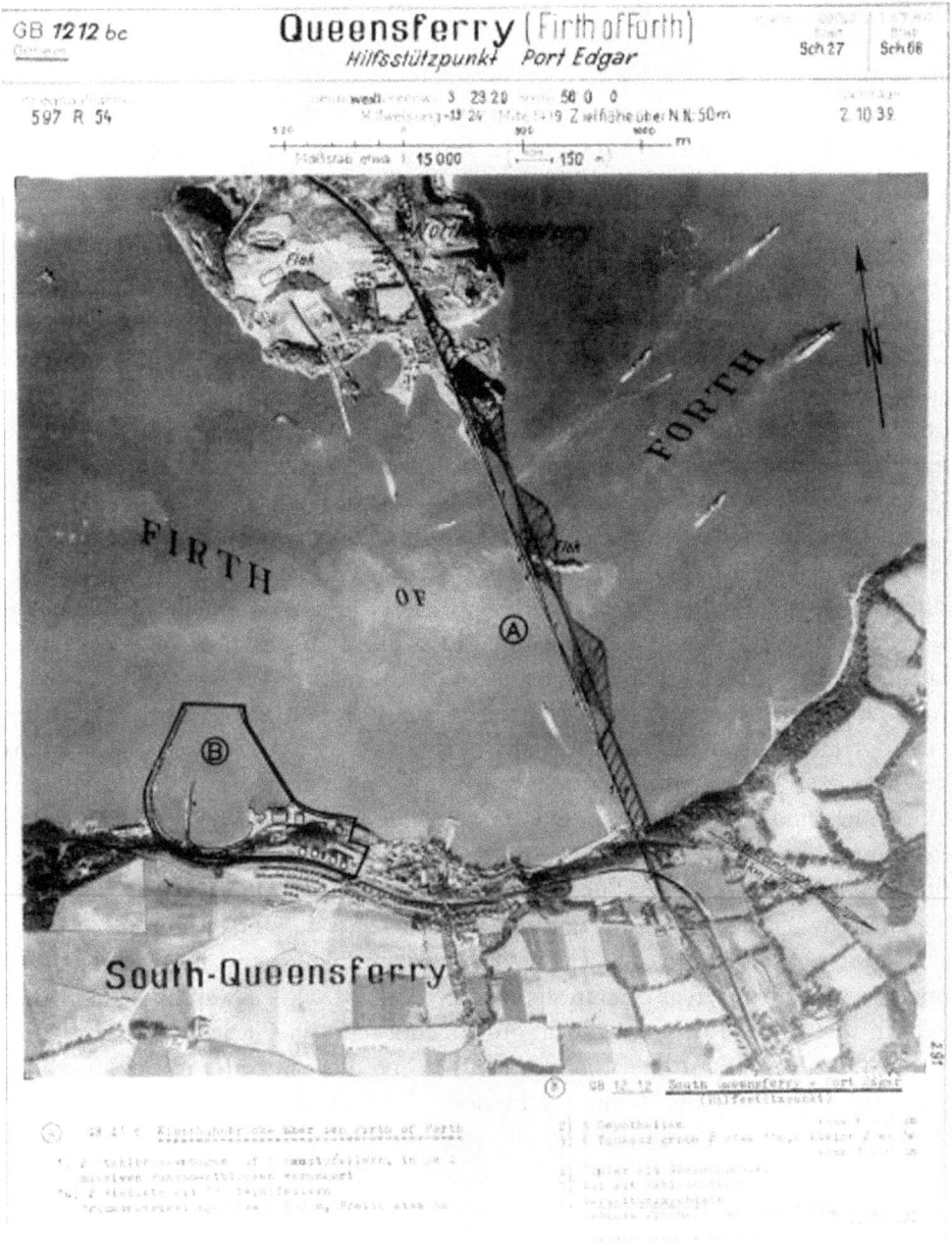

Figure 3. Page from German intelligence document detailing the Firth of Forth anchorages and showing a photograph taken on a Luftwaffe Arial reconnaissance of same taken during a reconnaissance mission on 02 October 1939. This photograph showed that the Royal Navy was using the anchorages for basing significant classes of warship – including what appears to be several cruisers and an aircraft carrier, probably HMS *Furious*.

In preparations for the planned campaign against British warships the German high command ordered aircraft reconnaissance of the Firth of Forth anchorages. One image, taken on a reconnaissance on 2 October 1939, is often misinterpreted as a photograph from an attacking aircraft on the 16th of the month. What the reconnaissance of the Firth of Forth on 2 October had shown the German High Command was that the anchorages adjacent to Rosyth were being used for significant classes of warships that would present suitable targets for air attack with a reduced risk of bombs landing on shore.[10] This would lead to the drawing up of a plan for such a strike operation to be flown at an opportune time. The plan of attack called for nine Ju.88 bombers of I/*Kampfgeschwader 30* to swoop in on the Firth of Forth in staggered formation and bomb any suitable warship targets laying at anchor off Rosyth. The date and time for the operation was set as the afternoon of 16 October 1939, this being the Luftwaffe's first plan for an air attack on the mainland United Kingdom.

Late 1930's defensive planning, that is up to 1938, for a major war with Germany adopted Rosyth, located in the Firth of Forth, as the main Royal Navy Home Fleet base, as had been the case towards the end of the 1914-1918 war. The reasoning behind advocating Rosyth as the main Home Fleet anchorage was that it was the most suitably located to counter German warships operating in the North Sea or perhaps venturing further northward to break out into the Atlantic Ocean or enter the Norwegian Sea. Even with the threat of air attack much greater than it had been in 1918, Rosyth was considered suitable as its air defenses – fighter aircraft, anti-aircraft guns and Chain Home RDF (Radio Direction Finding) stations, could be combined with those of Glasgow and Edinburgh, the major cities in central Scotland. This would relieve the RAF of the need to provide air defence for the north of the country, some 200 miles distant, reliving the burden on fighter squadrons.[11]

In 1938, following a reassessment of the problems and requirements for opposing German naval operations in the event of war, it was concluded that Rosyth was not the optimum location for countering a German warship break out to the Atlantic, a primary remit of the Home Fleet in order to safeguard the shipping routes to the United Kingdom. It was also clear that the 'long approaches [to the Forth anchorages] were vulnerable to mining, whereas the fierce tidal streams of the Pentland Firth afforded some protection to the main entrances to Scapa Flow' in the Orkney Isles.[12] Scapa Flow was also better

---

[10] British records show that such reconnaissance flights were not challenged by British fighter aircraft, the squadron defending the Forth, despite having some Spitfire I monoplane fighter aircraft on strength, was, in the first week of October 1939, operational with the obsolete Gloster Gladiator biplane fighter. This squadrons Operations Record Book Form 540 shows no operational flights on 02 October 1939

[11] S.W. Roskill, *History of the Second Word War, The War at Sea 1939-1945, Volume I: The Defensive*, United Kingdom Military Series, (London, HMSO, 1954), 77

situated to cut off German warships attempting to break into the Atlantic Ocean, but would be considerably more difficult to afford protection against air attack. It was decided to base the main fleet on Scapa Flow and the Home Fleet was centred there in the days leading up to the outbreak of war with Germany on 3 September 1939, although Rosyth would remain a significant anchorage and dockyard. In addition, the 15th Destroyer Flotilla, consisting of eight Destroyers and eight escort ships (all fitted with what was considered efficient AA armament), was based on Rosyth.[13]

At this early stage of the war the air defences for the Firth of Forth were in an embryonic state, with much left to be done to provide adequate defence against air attack. However, with a degree of A.A. (Anti-Aircraft) gun protection afforded by the 3rd Anti-Aircraft Division and the cover provided by two Spitfire I monoplane fighter Squadrons of the Royal Auxiliary Air Force, it was clear that any German bomber force operating over the Forth area, particularly in the vicinity of Rosyth, in daylight would have no easy task.[14] The two Royal Auxiliary Air Force Spitfire squadrons were the main defence against air attack during the hours of daylight, the Spitfire I being considered the most capable fighter aircraft in RAF service at that time. No. 602 (City of Glasgow) Squadron of the Royal Auxiliary Air Force had changed roles form army cooperation to fighter on 14 January 1939, being allocated to RAF No.12 Group.[15] On the change to a fighter role in 1939, the squadron had received some Gloster Gauntlet biplane fighters in lieu of Spitfire I monoplane fighters, the first of the latter arriving at RAF Abbotsinch (the modern day Glasgow International Airport), to the West of Glasgow, in May that year.[16] RAF Abbotsinch transferred from No.18 group Coastal Command to No.13 Group Fighter Command with effect from 13 September 1939.[17]

No. 602, along with No. 603 (City of Edinburgh) Squadron of the Royal Auxiliary Air Force, would constitute the main defence against air attack for

---

[12] Roskill, *The War at Sea 1939-1945, Volume I*, 77

[13] Roskill, *The War at Sea 1939-1945, Volume I*, 48

[14] A third Squadron allocated to the regions defence was equipped with Gloster Gladiator biplane fighters, considered obsolete against high speed monoplane bombers of the Ju.88 class

[15] No.602 City of Glasgow (Bombing) (Fighter) Squadron, Auxiliary Air Force, Form 540, Summary of Events for January 1939

No.602 City of Glasgow (Fighter) Squadron, Auxiliary Air Force, Form 540, Summary of Events for May 1939. No.602 Squadron was the first Royal Auxiliary Air Force squadron to be equipped with Spitfires

[17] No.602 Squadron, Form 540, Summary of Events, for September 1939

Central Scotland, nominally, as it was focused on the defence of the Firth of Forth. It was clear that deploying 602 Squadron nearer to the Firth of Forth would facilitate the ability to more effectively patrol areas where enemy aircraft threatening the Forth would be expected to transit through. For this reason, No.602 would be moved from Abbotsinch to RAF Drem in East Lothian, becoming operational from this field only on 13 October, three days before the German air raid on the 16th.[18] Prior to the move eastward, 602 Squadron would assist in the training of pilots of No.603 on the Spitfire I, which the latter squadron was to re-equip with. No.603 Squadron had re-rolled from a bomber role to a fighter role on 24 October 1938, but did not receive fighter aircraft, Gloster Gladiator biplanes, until late March 1939. Re-equipment with Spitfires commenced in mid-September 1939 when, on the 12th of the month, four pilots from 603 Squadron were instructed on the Spitfire I at Abbotsinch.[19] Re-equipment was still ongoing in mid-October when the squadron, based at RAF Turnhouse on the outskirts of the city of Edinburgh on the South shore of the Forth Estuary, engaged the German bombers attacking warships in the Forth on 16 October. Only on 11 October 1939 had No.603 Squadron handed over eight Gloster Gladiators to No.152 Squadron, another eight such aircraft being handed to No.141 Squadron on the 27th of the month as No.603 Squadron completed conversion to Spitfires.[20]

We know from operational records on both sides, local weather reports for the day and photographs of the raid in progress, that the weather in the area of the Forth Bridge was generally fine with patches of scattered low cloud and patches of haze in the wider Firth of Forth Estuary on the early afternoon of 16 October 1939.[21] The fine weather would be considered a double edged sword for the attacking force, making concealment harder, but making target identification and attack easier.

The range, some 600 or so km, each way, between Westerland on the North West German Island of Sylt and Rosyth in Scotland, made it desirable that the attacking force would operate from this advanced operating base, as aerodromes further south or South East would entail the burden of additional range related

---

[18] No.602 Squadron, Form 540, Summary of Events for October 1939. No.602 Squadron had moved to Grangemouth in early October, but, on 12 October, received orders to move to Drem, the move being effected the following morning

[19] No.602 Squadron, Form 540, Summary of Events, for September 1939

[20] No.603 Squadron, Form 541, Record of Events, Detail of Work Carried Out from 1430. hrs., 16/10/39 to 1630 hrs., 16/10/39

[21] No.602 Squadron, Form 540, Summary of Events, for October 1939

problems.[22] In the week following the raid on the Forth, British intelligence services indicated that one of the attacking aircraft had flown from Erfurt in Southern Germany with a refueling stop over at an advanced airfield in North West Germany.[23] However, this appears to have been nothing more than normal transfer of aircraft from one aerodrome to another.

Several values have bene put forward for the number of German aircraft involved in the operation - 9, 12, 15 - the latter coming from crew reports and German documentation, indicating the number of aircraft allocated to the operation, including reserves, the former apparently being the number of aircraft actually participating in the raid. Among the few details of the German raid provided in the 603 Squadrons Form 540 included that twelve aircraft were involved and 40 bombs were dropped in the vicinity of the anchorages near the Forth Bridge.[24] The Ju.88's had commenced take-off from Westerland at 11.00 hours for their two hour transit across the North Sea, cruise altitude being in the order of 13,000 ft.[25] The German attacking force, as would be the case for subsequent raids on shipping at sea and the air raid on Scapa Flow on the 17th, adopted a staggered loose formation of two and three aircraft.[26] Such formations, while being harder to detect, were more vulnerable to fighter attack once interception had been effected.

A No.602 operational document, 'Details of work carried out for 16 October' show that a total of 30 Spitfire I sorties were flown by the squadron that day. While no figures are available for operational hours flown by the Squadron on the 16th, a calculation of the airborne times for each sortie provides a value of 26 hours 40 minutes.[27] No.603 Squadron records for 16 October 1939 show that the Squadron flew 21 sorties in 14 hours 40 minutes

[22] This is not an exact distance and aircraft would not fly on a straight course line for the entire journey

[23] W.P. (39)101 Weekly Resume No.8 of the Naval, Military and Air Situation (12 noon, 19th October to 12 noon, 26th October, 1939. See also Paper No. C.O.8. (39)103

[24] Details on how many German aircraft operated in the vicinity of the Forth Bridge on 16 October are hazy at best – probably no more than six or seven - the exact number of bombs dropped in the Firth of Forth would have been somewhat less than forty

[25] The take-off time of 11.00 hours is taken to be Central European Time, which would have been 12.00 hours United Kingdom time in the Firth of Forth as Britain did not put its clocks back from British Summer Time to Greenwich Mean Time until 19 November 1939 and Germany observed Central European Time for the whole of 1939. The transit from Westerland to the Forth Estuary for the Ju.88 bombers was just over two hours

[26] W.P. (39)101 Weekly Resume No.8, 12 noon, 19th October to 12 noon, 26th October, 1939

[27] Data taken from No.602 Squadron document 'Details of work carried out for 16 October [1939]'

flying time during the course of the day's operations.[28] No.602 Squadrons higher sortie count can be explained by the fact that the squadron flew a number of those sorties during the course of the morning in response to several reports of enemy aircraft approaching, or over, the Forth area.

It was on the morning of the 16th that the first indications that an attack on the Firth of Forth was imminent came to light with British interceptions of German wireless signals that clearly indicated that such an attack against warships at Rosyth was in the offing.[29] Immediately, orders were drafted for the dispatch of No.607 (County of Durham) Fighter Squadron to move to Drem to reinforce the fighter squadrons covering Rosyth at that time - the above noted No.602 and No.603 Fighters squadrons.[30]

British records state that the raid commenced at 2.15 p.m.[31] Considering that the first alerts were not issued until the raid was in progress it is assumed that this recorded time is when the first German aircraft were on their bomb runs (dives) and the first of the guns of the 3rd Anti-Aircraft Division had opened fire.[32] The days Spitfire defensive operations had commenced before 10 am that morning when an unidentified aircraft overflew Drem airfield at 09.43 hours. Two minutes later, Blue Section of No.602 Squadron, three Spitfire I's, was ordered aloft to investigate and then conduct a patrol over the Isle of May at 5,000 ft., the aircraft lifting off from Drem at 09.49 hours.[33] At 10.11 hours, aircraft were reported to be flying East above the clouds at an altitude of 2,000 ft. At 10.23 hours, a message from Turnhouse was received at Drem, 'Blue Section have sighted and attacked enemy'.[34] The German aircraft, which had

---

[28] No.603 Squadron, Form 540, Summary of Events for 16 October 1939

[29] Richards, *The Royal Air Force 1939-1945, Vol. I*, 67

[30] C.O.S. (39) 51st Meeting, War Cabinet, Chiefs of Staff Committee, Minutes of Meeting held on 18th October, 1939, at 10..45 a.m., which refers to an additional squadron having been allocated to the defence of Rosyth, and the possibility of adding further squadrons was being looked at. See also Richards, *The Royal Air Force 1939-1945, Vol. I*, 67. Note: No.607 squadron was equipped with Gloster Gladiator biplane fighter aircraft in October 1939. This Squadron would not have been able to deploy for at least a day or two, even longer for much of the ground support

[31] War Cabinet (39) 50th, Conclusions of a Meeting of the War Cabinet held at 10 Downing Street, S.W., on Tuesday, October 17, 1939, at 11.30 A.M.

[32] Only a few guns opened fire initially as no air raid alert had been received, but these were followed by other guns after the alert had been given while the attack was in progress

[33] The No.602 Squadron Form 540 Summary of Events states 09.49, but the attached 'Detail of Work Carried Out' on the Form 540 for 16 October 1939, states 09.45 hours. This latter time probably refers to the time the aircraft were ordered into the air. The Isle of May (May Island) lies in the mouth of Forth Estuary some 25 km or so to the North East of Drem

been on a reconnaissance to determine the presence of suitable targets for the forthcoming bombing raid was, however, able to evade the Spitfires in cloud.[35] Twenty minutes later, Green Section was ordered aloft (the Spitfires took off from Drem two minutes later, Blue Section, which had taken off at 09.49 hours, recorded in records as landing at the same time) to investigate a report of two unidentified aircraft and then patrol over Dunbar at an altitude of 7,000 ft.[36] At 11.03 hours, Green Section was ordered to patrol over Drem at an altitude of 2,000 ft. Less than 20 minutes later an unidentified aircraft was reported over Drem by the Operations Centre at RAF Turnhouse. Red Section took off from Drem at 11.25 hours, but made no contact and was, at 11.37 hours, patrolling over Kinghorn.[37] Blue Section was ordered to patrol the area of St Abs Head at 11.39 hours, the section taking-off from Drem between 1142 and 1145 hours.[38] Having encountered no enemy aircraft Green Section landed at Drem at 11.59 hours, followed by Red Section, which landed at 12.18 hours then Blue Section, which landed at 12.45 hours – neither Red nor Blue Sections encountered enemy aircraft. At 13.26 hours, orders were received from the operations room at Turnhouse for Red Section to conduct a patrol over Crail at an altitude of 5,000 ft. (took off from Drem at 13.29 hours and landed back at Drem at 14.30 hours having not encountered any German aircraft) in response to reports that two aircraft were approaching from the East.[39] The 602 Squadron Form 540 states that Green Section, at 13.57 hours, landed at RAF Leuchars in Fife,

---

[34] No.602 Form 540, Summary of Events for 16 October 1939

[35] War Cabinet (39) 50th, Conclusions of a Meeting of the War Cabinet held at 10 Downing Street, S.W., on Tuesday, October 17, 1939, at 11.30 A.M. This German aircraft, by means of radio signal, would have been able to provide warning to the German bombing force of the presence of Spitfires in the target area, which was previously unknown to German intelligence. Unofficial statements that the bomber force crews were unaware of the presence of Spitfires, would, if occasioned in fact, point to a breakdown in communication between the various German departments

[36] No.602 Squadron, Form 540, Summary of Events for October 1939. Dunbar lies on the South shore of the Firth of Forth around 10 km or so to the East of Drem

[37] No.602 Squadron, Form 540, Summary of Events for October 1939. Kinghorn is a small coastal town lying on the North shore of the Forth Estuary about 7 km or so to the Northeastward of the City of Edinburgh, which lies on the South shore

[38] No.602 Squadron, Form 540, Summary of Events for October 1939. St Abs Head lies on the Scottish East coast about 30 km or so to the South East of Drem

[39] No.602 Squadron, Form 540, Summary of Events for October 1939. Crail lies on the North shore of the Forth Estuary about 20 km in a northerly direction from Drem

North of the Forth Estuary, having received orders to this effect from the operations centre at RAF Turnhouse.[40] However, there is no mention in the Form 540 of Green Section having taken off from Drem following its landing from an earlier patrol.

Figure 4. An iconic portrayal of a Supermarine Spitfire MK.I single-engine monoplane fighter aircraft in summer 1940. This was representative of the Spitfires employed by 602 and 603 Squadrons in the skies over the Firth of Forth in East central Scotland in October 1939. CC

---

[40] No.602 Squadron, Form 540, Summary of Events for October 1939. RAF Leuchars was a Coastal Command air station located about three kilometers North of St Andrews on the Scottish East coast

Figure 5. *I/Kampfgeschwader 30* conducted moderate angle dive attacks on the British warships in the Forth Estuary as this form of attack was unquestionably more accurate than level bombing. This was of paramount importance in order to reduce the risk of civilian casualties in line with the rules of engagement then in force. CC

Blue Section of 'B' Flight took off from Drem at 14.23 hours to conduct a patrol over Dalkeith at an altitude of 30,000 ft.[41] This was followed by Yellow Section, which took off at 14.34 hours to patrol over Turnhouse at an altitude of 10,000 ft. Not long after getting airborne Blue Section, at this point flying at 6,000 ft. on a North heading, encountered two German Ju.88 bombers at 4,000 ft. altitude and 90 deg. flying in an easterly direction some five miles to the East of the Isle of May in the Forth Estuary.[42] The Spitfires were able to deliver two attacks between 14.35 hours and 14.50 hours, by which time the aircraft were to the North East of St. Abbs Head. At least two of the Spitfire pilots stated that there was no return fire from the German aircraft during the first attack from above and rear of the German aircraft, but that tracer fire was observed coming from the bombers during the second attack. The Spitfires opened fire at around 400 yards down to 300 yards firing several bursts of 0.303 inch machine gun fire (F/O. Webb, states 'Four burst representing 10 seconds fire'), but no hits were recorded on the German aircraft, which took advantage of available cloud in evading Spitfires and dived almost to sea level.[43]

Having lost the German aircraft due to cloud cover following the first attack, another German aircraft was sighted flying at sea level at 14.50 hours. This Ju.88 was attacked by a Spitfire from Blue Section, which was put into 'a steep turning dive'. The Spitfire opened fire at 350 yards down to 200 yards in a single eight second burst against the Ju.88, which was noted to be conducting slow left and right turns in order to throw off the Spitfire pilots aim. The Spitfire pilot noted some smoke appearing from the direction of the Ju.88 starboard engine before the attack was broken off due to expenditure of all ammunition.[44] This aircraft may well have been the Ju.88 commanded by Lieutenant Horst von Riesen that was damaged in the starboard engine by an anti-aircraft shell during the attack on a warship, probably the Destroyer HMS *Mohawk*. Riesen's damaged Ju.88 was able to make it back to Westerland. As Blue Section was engaging a second German aircraft (this may have been the same aircraft observed twice) Red Section got back into the air (take off time being 14.51 hours) and was ordered to patrol over Drem at 10,000 ft. to cover the return of the other Sections.

---

[41] No.602 Squadron, Form 540, Summary of Events for October 1939. Note. The various Form F Combat Reports for this Section states take-off time as 14.25, two minutes later than the squadron Form 540. Dalkeith lies a few km to the South East of the City of Edinburgh

[42] These aircraft were erroneously reported as He.111 bombers in the 602 Squadron Form F Combat Reports provided by the pilots. The altitude and headings of the Spitfires and German bombers is given in the same Form F combat reports

[43] No.602 Squadron, Form F Combat Reports for 16 October 1939. The German aircraft were noted to have went down to as low as 20 ft. above the sea surface in order to evade the Spitfire attacks

[44] No.602 Squadron, Form F Combat Report, 16.10.1939 (F/O. Webb)

Following their respective interceptions of enemy aircraft, Blue, Yellow, Red and Green Sections of 602 Squadron landed back at Drem at 15.15, 15.21, 15.21 and 16.20 hours respectively.[45]

Around the time Blue Section of 602 Squadron was engaging the German aircraft to the North East of the Isle of May, No.603 Squadron joined the defensive fighter operation. Spitfire I's, L1070, L1050 and L1061, of Red Section of 'A' Flight, No.603 Squadron, had taken off from Turnhouse at 14.30 hours, followed five minutes later by three Spitfire I's, L1067, L1049 and L1048, of Yellow Section. Not long after getting airborne, Yellow Section encountered three German Ju.88 bombers in loose formation. These, on observing the Spitfires, scattered and evaded the British fighter aircraft in cloud, but not before each of the German aircraft had been fired upon with no noticeable effect. There was some return fire from at least one of the German aircraft. A Spitfire I, L1048 (pilot P/O. G.K. Gilroy), was struck by a single rifle calibre bullet which went through the upper engine cover.[46] A short time later, 14.45 hours, Red Section of 603 Squadron intercepted a Ju.88 to the East of Dalkeith at an altitude of 4,000 ft.[47] This aircraft was subjected to attack and was shot down, falling into the sea off Port Seton.[48] Pilot reports indicated that the Spitfires were flying in a 'wide VIC formation' and, at the time the enemy aircraft was sighted, were in the process of moving their patrol area to Dalkeith from the previous position over Haddington.[49] The German aircraft and the Spitfires were approaching each other head on. On observing the Spitfires, the German pilot turned to port, the Spitfires then moving into line astern in a starboard turn. The lead Spitfire dived toward the target and positively identified it as a German bomber, upon which the pilot ordered the other fighters to open fire, all three Spitfires carrying out successive No.1 attacks from slightly above the German Ju.88 bomber.[50] In an attempt to escape, the Ju.88 was dived ground-ward and headed for the coast, which was crossed at an altitude of around 1,000 ft. Once over the sea, the German pilot flew down to about 50 ft.

[45] No.602 Squadron, Form 540, Summary of Events for October 1939

[46] No.603 Squadron, Form 541, Record of Events for 16 October 1939

[47] This aircraft was initially identified by the 603 Squadron Spitfire pilots as a He.111, then a Do.217. No.603 Squadron, Form F Combat Report, 16.10.1939 (F/Lt. Gifford). The Ju.88 is thought to have been one of those previously intercepted by Yellow Section

[48] No.603 Squadron, Form 541, Record of Events for 16 October 1939. Port Seten lies on the South shore of the Forth Estuary about 5 km East of the City of Edinburgh

[49] No.603 Squadron, Form F Combat Report, 16.10.1939 (F/Lt. Gifford). Haddington lies about 10 km or so East of the City of Edinburgh and about 7 or 8 km inland from the Forth Estuary

[50] No.603 Squadron Form F Combat Report, 16.10.1939 (F/Lt. Gifford)

above the waves as he tried to throw off his pursuers, but also executed at least one gentle turn manoeuvre, considered to have been to afford a better firing solution for the Ju.88 upper gunner. As each Spitfire broke away after a firing pass the German pilot conducted steeper turns, allowing the upper gunner to better engage the fighters. However, as each of the Spitfires broke-away after a firing pass, another fighter would conduct its attack, presumably having a detrimental effect on the German gunners aim. Typically the Spitfire's opened fire at 350 yards down to 50 yards in roughly four second bursts. The effect of such concentrations of 0.303 inch machine gun fire resulted in a number of pieces of the fuselage detaching from the Ju.88, these noted to cover an area of 'about two to three feet in front of the tail unit'.[51] During the Section Leaders second attack he 'adjusted his deflection to ensure hits in the vulnerable parts of the fuselage'.[52] Following this attack the Ju.88 hit the sea and was seen by the Spitfire pilots to break-up. Three of the crew of four were rescued from the sea by a British fishing boat.[53] Following the air combats, Red and Yellow Sections landed at Turnhouse between 14.55 hours and 15.00 hours.[54]

Another Section of 603 Squadron Spitfires had taken off from Turnhouse between 14.30 and 14.45 hours and patrolled North Berwick and then moved to cover Rosyth.[55] No German aircraft were encountered and the section landed back at Turnhouse between 15.20 (the single aircraft that took off at 14.30 hours) and 16.00 hours (the two Spitfires that took-off at 14.45 hours).[56] A fourth Section of 603 Squadron Spitfires had taken off at 14.45 hours. Two aircraft of the section did not encounter any German aircraft, but the third, Spitfire, L1046, after, it was claimed by the pilot, F/O. J.C. Boulter, becoming detached from the rest of the section, attacked a German aircraft erroneously identified as a He.111 (this would have been a Ju.88) heading away from Aberdour in an easterly direction.[57] The attack produced no notable results

[51] No.603 Squadron, Form F Combat Report, 16.10.1939 (F/Lt. Gifford)

[52] No.603 Squadron, Form F Combat Report, 16.10.1939 (F/Lt. Gifford)

[53] No.603 Form 541, Record of Events for 16 October 1939. See also No.603 Squadron Form F Combat Report, 16.10.1939 (F/Lt. Gifford), which records the crash as having occurred around 2 miles from Port Seaton, the position certainly being somewhere in the region of 2 to 5 miles from Port Seaton. There is disagreement between sources as to what aircraft this was. Some published sources state this was the aircraft of the Gruppe commander, Pohl, and that he was the only survivor of the four crew. However, British government records clearly show three survivors, refuting the aforementioned claim

[54] No.603 Squadron, Form 541, Record of Events for 16 October 1939

[55] No.603 Squadron, Form 541, Record of Events for 16 October 1939. North Berwick lies about 15 km North easterly from the City of Edinburgh

[56] No.603 Squadron, Form 541, Record of Events for 16 October 1939

before it was broken off, apparently due to a thick haze, observability being further reduced due to the effects of the sun.

Two Spitfires from 603 Squadron, L1050 from, Red Section and L1049 from Yellow Section, took off from Turnhouse at 15.40 and 16.00 hours respectively. A single Ju.88 was intercepted over Rosyth flying at very low altitude.[58] In the ensuing attack by at least one Spitfire the German aircraft was 'pursued out to sea with the starboard engine not running and return fire from the rear gunner suspended'.[59] The Spitfire from yellow Section landed back at Turnhouse at 16.15 hours and the aircraft from Red Section landed at 16.30 hours.[60] At 15.56 hours Blue Section of 602 Squadron took off from Drem to conduct a patrol over the Forth Bridge at an altitude of 14,000 ft., landing back at Drem at 17.04 hours without encountering any enemy aircraft. The last of the squadron patrols that day was conducted by Red Section, which took off from Drem at 17.45 hours with orders to patrol over Leven at 2,000 ft., landing back at Drem at 17.55 hours without encountering enemy aircraft.[61]

During the course of the days combats No.603 Squadron expended 16,000 rounds of 0.303 inch ammunition.[62] No form has been found in the archives detailing No.602 Squadrons 0.303 inch ammunition expenditure during the day's operations.

In the governmental official history of the air war Squadron Leader E.E. Stevens from No.603 (City of Edinburgh) Fighter Squadron was credited with the first German aircraft to be shot down by RAF Fighter Command during World War II.[63] However, there is no mention in either the No.603 Squadron Summary of Events or Record of Events for 16 October 1939, of a Squadron

---

[57] No.603 Squadron, Form 541, Record of Events for 16 October 1939. Aberdour lies about 7 km North easterly from Rosyth on the North shore of the Forth Estuary

[58] No.603 Squadron, Form 541, Record of Events for 16 October 1939. This was probably the aircraft mentioned in the official history being chased at rooftop height. See also Richards, *The Royal Air Force 1939-1945, Vol. I*, 67

[59] No.603 Squadron, Form F Combat Report, 16.10.1939

[60] No.603 Squadron, Form 541, Record of Events for 16 October 1939. It is unclear from data within the squadron From 541 to determine if both Spitfires participated in this attack or if only one such aircraft participated. The Rosyth anchorages lie almost in the shadow of the Forth Rail Bridge

[61] No.603 Squadron, Form 541, Record of Events for 16 October 1939. Leven lies about 25 km North easterly from Rosyth on the North shore of the Forth Estuary

[62] No.603 Squadron, Summary, from 1435. hrs., 22/10/39 to 1525 hrs., 22/10/39

[63] Richards, *The Royal Air Force 1939-1945, Vol. I*, 82

Leader E.E. Stevens flying operational sorties during the course of the day's operations. It has not been possible to locate a Form F combat record for 16 October in the National Archives at Kew for a Squadron Leader Stevens on the 16th October 1939, either with 603 or 602 Squadron. No.602 Squadron summary of events record confirm that no pilot with the rank and name of Squadron Leader E.E. Stevens flew sorties on 16 October 1939. It has not been possible to locate a record of events for 602 Squadron for October 1939 in the National Archives at Kew. The 692 Squadron Form 541, Record of Events for 16 October clearly shows the German aircraft that was shot down by the squadron that day as falling to the guns of the Spitfires of Red Section, (Spitfire L1070 flown by F/Lt. P. Gifford, L1050 flown by P/O. C. Robertson and L0161 flown by F/O. H.K. Macdonald).[64] In the absence of any records evidence it seems reasonable to form an assumption that the official history is wrong in its determination of what pilot was responsible for the destruction of the first German aircraft by a fighter aircraft of Fighter Command in World War II.

We know from detailed analysis of operational records that this was not the case, certainly in regards to the two Ju.88's shot down that day falling to the guns of Spitfire's of 603 Squadron and 602 Squadron – P. Gifford of 603 and G. Pinkerton of 602 being credited with shooting the German aircraft down. These were the pilots attacking when the respective German aircraft went down, but it should be remembered that the German aircraft were subjected to multiple attacks by multiple Spitfires, a number of which would have inflicted damage of various degrees of severity. Pinkerton is also credited with conducting the first attack on a German aircraft by an aircraft of Fighter Command when he intercepted, without success, a German reconnaissance aircraft on the morning of 16 October 1939. Only a single Spitfire is noted to have been damaged, as previously noted, L1048 of 602 Squadron being hit by a single bullet fired from a Ju.88 defensive gun, this being the first incidence of a Fighter Command aircraft suffering combat damage during World War II.

The guns of the 3rd Anti-Aircraft Division, tasked with the defence of Rosyth and the Forth Bridge, fired 104 rounds during the air raid on 16 October 1939.[65] While reports of the time that at least one Ju.88 bomber was shot down by AA guns were erroneous, one Ju.88 may have been damaged, this being the aircraft subsequently shot down by Spitfires of 603 Squadron.[66] The failure of the guns

---

[64] No.603 Squadron, Form 541, Record of Events for 16 October 1939

[65] War Cabinet (39) 50th, Conclusions of a Meeting of the War Cabinet, October 17, 1939

[66] It is not possible to conclusively determine if this aircraft was indeed damaged as a result of surface anti-aircraft fire or if the aircraft suffered a structural problem when put into a dive - a common problem with early Ju.88 bombers

to bring down any of the attacking aircraft was a cause for concern for the Chiefs of Staff, which would lead to proposals for a significant increase in the AA gun defences covering Rosyth. In his dispatch, 'The Anti-Aircraft Defence of the United Kingdom, From 28 July 1939, to 15 April 1945' the head of AA Command, General Pile, concluded that the equipment and the training of the personnel of his command were not up to the standards that were required for modern warfare.[67] In his Dispatch, General Pile went on to note 'it was at once apparent that peacetime training was insufficient and existing equipment was insufficient to deal entirely successfully with wartime targets, which continually dived and turned and flew at comparatively high speeds. Steps were taken to have alterations designed and made to meet the needs of the situation, but nearly two years elapsed before these were actually produced'.[68]

Initially it was claimed that no less than four German aircraft had been shot down during the raid on the Forth on 16 October. We now know from documented evidence that only two such aircraft were shot down – both, as noted above, lost to Spitfires - and a third was destroyed when it succumbed to damage inflicted during an interception by Spitfire fighters and crashed in Holland.

The results of the raid(s) was minor damage to two Royal Navy Light Cruisers and a Destroyer. One bomb struck the Cruiser HMS *Southampton*, laying at anchor to the North West of the Forth Bridge, but the ship had the good fortune to have the bomb pass straight through three deck levels and exit out of her side without exploding. The bomb, determined in damage assessment reports to be a 1000 kg class delay action fuse weapon, but probably a smaller 500 kg or 250 kg class weapon, 'struck the corner of the pom [anti-aircraft gun mount] magazine, port side 87 station, penetrated three decks, passed out through the ships side, and exploded below the water line. Structural damage was caused in the path of the bomb and electrical power failed temporarily'.[69] The limited damage inflicted included the sinking of the admiral's barge, which was berthed alongside the cruiser. Casualties amounted to one person killed and seven wounded.

---

[67] See also Survey of the A.A. Defence of the United Kingdom, Vol. II, 154 and Collier, *The Defence of the United Kingdom*, 82

[68] The Anti-Aircraft Defence of the United Kingdom, From 28 July 1939, to 15 April 1945, Supplement to the London Gazette, The War Office, 1947, 5976

[69] B.R.186(2) ([initially C.B. 4273 (52)], H.M. Ships Damaged or Sunk by Enemy Action, 3rd Sept. 1939 to 2nd Sept. 1945 (1952)

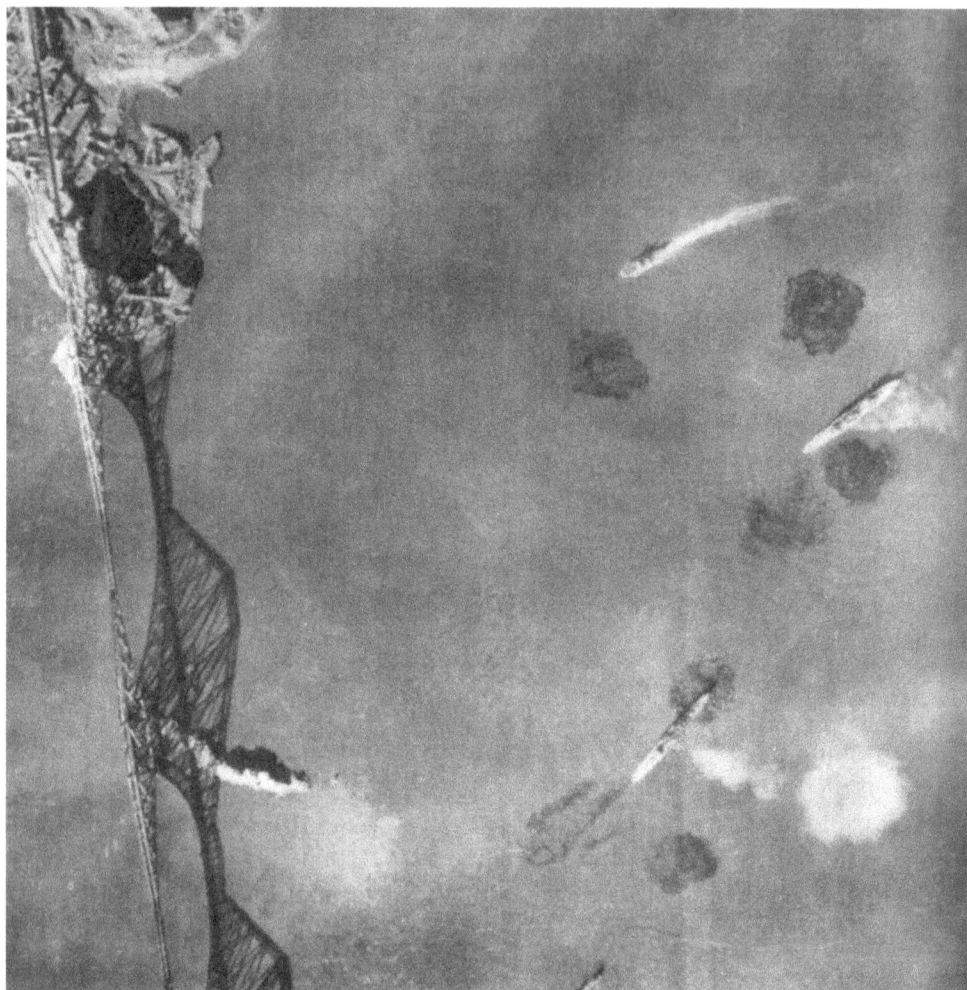

Figure 6. The best available photograph of the air attack on the British warships in progress shows the Light Cruisers *Southampton* and the *Edinburgh* at anchor with bomb blast scarring on the water surface. The ship at the top of the photograph, at times mistaken for the Destroyer *Mohawk*, is clearly underway on a north easterly to south westerly heading, adjacent to bomb scarring left by a Ju.88 aircraft's bomb attack on a cruiser.

Several bombs landed near the Light Cruiser HMS *Edinburgh*, also at anchor to the North West of the Forth Bridge. This caused some minor damage and killed one and injured six crew.[70] The two near miss direct action fuse 500 kg or

[70] B.R.186(2), H.M. Ships Damaged or Sunk by Enemy Action. This is often stated as a single bomb, based on initial reports, but later analysis showed that two near missies and a third, 'counter mined' bomb landed in close proximity to HMS *Edinburgh*. See also Roskill, *The War at Sea -1945, Volume I*, 75, which erroneously mentions damage only to the Light Cruiser HMS *Southampton* and a Destroyer (*Mohawk*)

250 kg class bombs 'counter mined a third [bomb] 20 ft. above the water and about 50 ft. from the starboard side (40-46 stations). Minor structural and electrical damage was caused mainly by splinters'.[71]

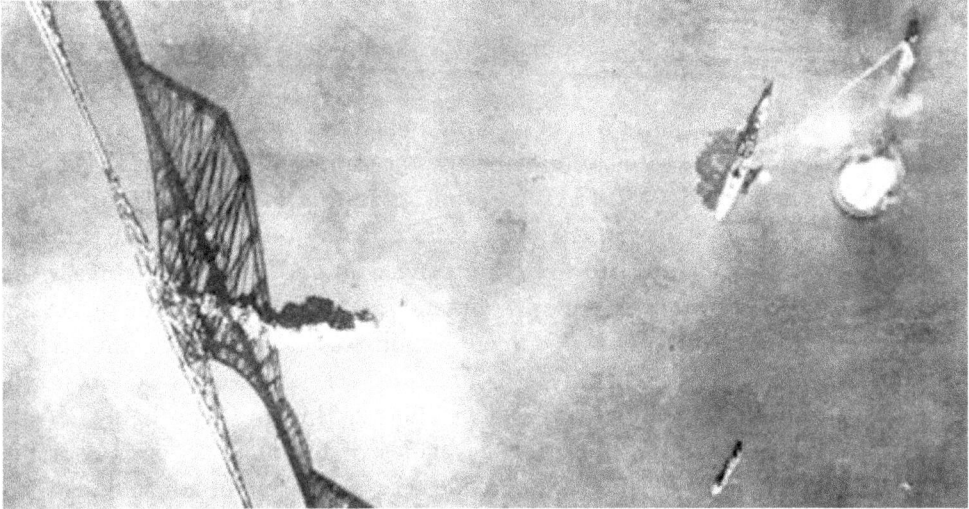

Figure 7. A bomb, released from a Ju.88, explodes in the water a reasonably safe distance from a Royal Navy Light Cruiser at anchor off Rosyth on 02 October 1939.

The fighting efficiency of HMS *Southampton* was impaired, the vessel requiring three days temporary repairs, while the fighting efficiency of the *Edinburgh* was not impaired. The damage inflicted on the *Southampton* and the *Edinburgh* led to recommendations for the introduction, or improvement, of 'splinter protection to exposed personnel etc., and also the following electrical items: Breakers to be locked in the "on" position; Starter handles to L.P. generators to be locked in the "on" position; important fuzes to be wired in'.[72]

Primary source documentation and much secondary source material details that another bomb exploded in the water close to the Tribal Class Destroyer HMS *Mohawk* causing the largest number of casualties of the raid - 16 killed and 44 wounded (the Captain of the ship was amongst the fatalities) and minor superficial splinter damage to the ship.[73] However, the most reliable information available from conflicting documentation proves beyond contestation that the *Mohawk* departed Harwich on North Sea convoy escort duties on 14 October 1939. While she is well documented as arriving in the Firth of Forth on the 16th,

---

[71] B.R.186(2), H.M. Ships Damaged or Sunk by Enemy Action

[72] B.R.186(2), H.M. Ships Damaged or Sunk by Enemy Action

[73] Richards, *The Royal Air Force 1939-1945, Vol. I*, 67

her position and status at the time of the air attack - at anchor or underway - has proved harder to verify. While much of the primary documentation and secondary source material would imply, or at the very least direct the reader in such a manner as to infer, that the *Mohawk* was at anchor in the vicinity of the Forth Bridge, more detailed analysis of naval documentation paints a completely different picture. This alternative view shows the *Mohawk* underway about one and a half miles from the Isle of May, a not inconsiderable ~50 km (~31 miles) from the Rosyth and Forth Bridge vicinity, when she was attacked by one or more Ju.88 bombers. This is supported by an important Admiralty document B.R.186(2), which reads 'MOHAWK, while escorting a convoy 1 and a half miles from May Island, was attacked by aircraft. Both bombs fell about 45 ft. to starboard, one abreast the break of the forecastle and the other abreast the torpedo tubes. Damage caused by splinters was considerable but structural damage was not serious'.[74] This document continued that it was determined that the bombs were either 'direct action [contact] or very short delay action fuzed' weapons of undetermined size [500 kg or 1000 kg, but most probably 250 kg class].[75] As well as suffering the most casualties of the day's air raids over the Forth Estuary, *Mohawk* suffered considerable impairment to her fighting efficiency. Damage occurred in the H.A. (High Angle) rangefinder with the result that 'practically all control and gun circuits were put out of action'.[76] The extent of the damage resulted in *Mohawk* being out of action for two months.[77]

Other than the major surface unit in dry dock at Rosyth, the 15 inch gun Battlecruiser HMS *Hood*, there were, of course, other warships in the Firth of Forth at the time of the attack, including the Polish Submarine *Orzel*. The *Orzel* had, following a hazardous journey through the Baltic Sea from Tallinn, arrived in the Firth of Forth on 14 October.[78] Completely overlooked in accounts of the defensive actions in the Firth of Forth region on the of 16th October 1939 is a depth charge attack on a suspected U-boat by the destroyer HMS *Afridi* and the Sloop HMS *Hastings*.[79] We know from German records, however, that no

---

[74] B.R.186(2), H.M. Ships Damaged or Sunk by Enemy Action

[75] B.R.186(2), H.M. Ships Damaged or Sunk by Enemy Action

[76] B.R.186(2), H.M. Ships Damaged or Sunk by Enemy Action

[77] B.R.186(2), H.M. Ships Damaged or Sunk by Enemy Action

[78] W.P. 39(94). (Also paper No. C.O.S. (39)92). War Cabinet. Weekly Resume No.7 of the Naval, Military and Air Situation (12 Noon, 12th October to 12 Noon, 19th October, 1939). Tallinn lies on the Estonian Baltic coast

[79] W.P. 39(94). (Also paper No. C.O.S. (39)92). War Cabinet. Weekly Resume No.7 of the Naval, Military and Air Situation (12 Noon, 12th October to 12 Noon, 19th October, 1939). HMS *Afridi* had constituted part of the 4th Destroyer Flotilla of the Mediterranean Fleet that had returned to UK waters earlier in October 1939. *Afridi* was not, however, operating as part of the

U-boat was in the area at the time, the depth charge attack, which was conducted against a phantom target or perhaps an unfortunate marine mammal, resulting from a heightened state of alert following the loss, to torpedo attack, of the battleship *HMS Royal Oak* at Scapa Flow a few days previous.

A controversial issue resulting from the raid was the fact that the early warning system for the Firth of Forth area did not work as planned, no air raid sirens sounding for the public, nor was there any warning for the local defences. The A.A. Gun Operations Room received literally no advanced warning that enemy aircraft were approaching. In fact, the first indication that a raid was underway was when some of the local defence guns of the 3rd Anti-Aircraft Division opened fire, the crews aware that an attack was underway when the Ju.88's commenced diving toward their targets – the Light Cruisers HMS *Edinburgh* and *Southampton* at anchor off Rosyth.[80]

The failure of the defences to detect the incoming raid and provide a warning would be the subject of debate at both military and political levels in the days and weeks following the raid. Following a quick investigation it was determined that the lack of early warning of the air raid was due to a malfunction of the power apparatus in the local R.D.F. (Radio Direction Finding) station covering the approach to the Forth area.[81] Headquarters RAF Fighter Command had become aware of the raid from the Admiralty only after the attack had actually commenced, but it was pointed out that 'fighter patrols were already in the air'.[82] Post war it was stated that the warning radar covering the area had failed that morning due to 'a failure of the power apparatus', allowing the German bombers to approach the target area without being detected.[83]

4th Destroyer Flotilla, which had in effect been dispersed. HMS *Hastings* was allocated to the loosely termed Rosyth Escort Force in September 1939 and deployed in early October that year

[80] Collier, *The Defence of the United Kingdom*, 154

[81] War Cabinet (39) 50th, Conclusions of a Meeting of the War Cabinet, October 17, 1939. See also Richards, *The Royal Air Force 1939-1945, Vol. I*, 82. R.D.F. (Radio Direction Finding), part of the 'Chain Home' radar warning system

[82] War Cabinet (39) 50th, Conclusions of a Meeting of the War Cabinet, October 17, 1939. The Spitfire patrol that was in the air at the commencement of the attack was Blue Section of No.602 City of Glasgow Squadron

[83] Richards, *The Royal Air Force 1939-1945, Vol. I*, 82

Figure 8. A typical Chain Home RDF (radar) farm. CC

Post war official writings on the subject appeared to downplay the failure of the warning system, in regards to public air raid sirens not sounding, in that no raid on a town actually took place. 'The silence of the public air-raid sirens could be justified on the ground that no attack on the mainland was expected, or in fact took place' read the official history of the defence of the United Kingdom.[84] There was, however, no way to try to downplay the lack of warning of the raid given to the local Gun Operations Room. As noted above, the warning of attack was received momentarily after the attack actually commenced, at which point those available anti-aircraft guns that had not already done so, without the order, opened fire as German aircraft appeared over the Forth Bridge and anchorage adjacent to Rosyth. One of the defensive gun positions (undisclosed at what site) was undergoing gunnery practice with drill rounds when the attack commenced, delaying its being brought to bear on the enemy aircraft as the drill ammunition had to be replaced by live ammunition.[85] While the attack was in progress, no one sounded the public air raid sirens, this being defended by the statement that 'as the raid was already in progress, the Air Officer Commanding-in-Chief had decided not to issue an air raid warning'.[86]

---

[84] Collier, *The Defence of the United Kingdom*, .82

[85] Collier, *The Defence of the United Kingdom*, .82

[86] War Cabinet (39) 50th, Conclusions of a Meeting of the War Cabinet, October 17, 1939

Figure 9. Although Chain Home RDF would prove of paramount importance in the dark days of the Battle of Britain in summer 1940, a power unit failure neutralized its effectiveness during the German air raid on the Forth Estuary on 16 October 1939. CC

The day after the raid took place there was a debate within the Chiefs of Staff Committee as to 'whether, if an attack developed before an air raid warning had been issued, it was nevertheless desirable to issue a warning. It was generally agreed that it was desirable to do so. Failure to do so in this instance [the raid on the 16th] had in fact resulted in a number of people being exposed to unnecessary risk'.[87] This statement was at odds with some media reports of the time that no warning had been given as it was known that no raid on land was probable, this fallacious view surviving through the decades into the twenty first century. It is a point of fact that the day after the Raid on the Forth, an air raid warning was sounded in the Forth and the Humber due to the suspected presence of German reconnaissance aircraft and the fact that information had been received of an air raid in progress at Scapa Flow.[88] Further, on 23 October 1939, an air raid warning was sounded in the general Firth of Forth area. The events that led to this alert stemmed from a signal that was sent out from the sloop HMS *Grimsby*, which was anchored under the Forth Bridge, reporting that '5 enemy aircraft had passed over, moving west'.[89] The message was received at the Admiralty before being passed on to RAF Fighter Command. Although Fighter Command, with confidence, suspected that the aircraft were British, an alert was issued. This incident would result in recommendations that an alert from an observation of this nature should not be issued unless the aircraft were confirmed as hostile or were actually in the process of attacking surface targets.[90]

As well as a warning failure there was, perhaps less serious in that it did not prevent aircraft being engaged, a major failure in identification of the type of German aircraft involved. British governmental documents stated that the German bombers, mistaken as He.111 and Do.215s, were engaged by three Auxiliary Air Force squadrons, two armed with Spitfires and one with Gladiators.'[91] However, although a Gladiator Squadron was based to cover the South and central regions of Scotland, only the two Spitfire Squadrons made contact with German aircraft on the 16th. The pilots of these two Spitfire squadrons erroneously identified the German aircraft as Heinkel He.111's.[92]

---

[87] War Cabinet (39) 50th, Conclusions of a Meeting of the War Cabinet, October 17, 1939

[88] War Cabinet (39) 50th, Conclusions of a Meeting of the War Cabinet, October 17, 1939. The Humber is a tidal estuary located on England's East coast several hundred km south of the Forth Estuary

[89] C.O.S. (39) 57th Meeting, War Cabinet, Chiefs of Staff Committee, Minutes of Meeting held on 24th October, 1939, at 10..45 a.m. HMS *Grimsby*, which had recently arrived in the Firth of Forth from China, was sunk in 1941

[90] C.O.S. (39) 57th Meeting, Chiefs of Staff Committee, 24th October, 1939

[91] War Cabinet (39) 50th, Conclusions of a Meeting of the War Cabinet, October 17, 1939

[92] A decade and a half after the event, the German aircraft were officially referred to as 'Junkers

A British intelligence gain from the raid on the Firth of Forth came from statements from captured German aircrew, in particular the commander of the German raiding force whom stated that 'his orders forbade him to attack the Forth Bridge or ships in berth'.[93] This was the first real confirmation that the Germans were observing a similar policy to that of Britain – avoiding attacking targets that unduly risked causing civilian casualties. This, of course, was a policy that would end, as would that of Great Britain's similar policy, once the period known as the 'Phoney War' ended in summer 1940.[94] A German intelligence gain was confirmation that the Firth of Forth was defended by one or more Spitfire fighter squadrons and that the anti-aircraft defence for Rosyth had proved to be ineffective.

News of the air raid on the warships in the Firth of Forth was not sent out to War Cabinet ministers until 6.30 pm on the evening of 16 October 1939.[95] The following day, Air Chief Marshal Sir Hugh Dowding, C.C.V.O., K.C.B., C.M.G., A.D.C., Air Officer Commanding in Chief, Fighter Command, sent a short note to the Spitfire squadrons involved in the previous days operations – 'First blood to the Auxiliaries'.[96] Despite the upbeat tone of this note it would soon become clear that the air raid on the Firth of Forth and a subsequent air raid on Scapa Flow the following day, together with the sinking of the *Royal Oak* at Scapa Flow by the submarine U-47 several days previous, had a profound short-term impact on British defence policy much greater than that which can be measured from the material losses – an old Battleship sunk, damage to a decommissioned battleship being utilised as a depot ship and minor damage to a few Light Cruisers and a Destroyer.[97] While casualties could be considered to be light for the air attacks on the Firth of Forth and at Scapa Flow, the casualties that resulted from the torpedoing of the *Royal Oak* were unfortunately very high – 810 killed.[98]

---

88 bombers' in the first volume of the British official histories of the War at Sea – Roskill, *The War at Sea 1939-1945, Volume I*, 75. As noted in the main body, the Gladiator squadron stationed in Scotland took no part in the days operations

[93] War Cabinet (39) 51, Conclusions of a Meeting of the War Cabinet held at 10 Downing Street, S.W., on Wednesday, October 18, 1939, at 11.30 A.M.

[94] This is a term used to refer to the war period from September 1940 until the major German offensive against France and the Low Countries on 10 May 1940, although there were, of course, ground, air and sea campaigns fought during this period

[95] C.O.S. (39) 50th Meeting, War Cabinet, Chiefs of Staff Committee, Minutes of Meeting held on 17th October, 1939, at 10..45 A.M.

[96] No.602 Squadron, Form 540, Summary of Events for October 1939

[97] The air raid on Scapa Flow on 17 October damaged, by two bomb near miss's, the depot ship (former battleship) HMS *Iron Duke* – casualties were 1 killed and 24 treated for shock

Politically and militarily the vulnerability of warships to submarine and air attack was unacceptable and measures would be put in place to secure the anchorages of the Firth of Forth and at Scapa Flow against submarine and air attack.[99] However, the effect of the attacks of the 14th, 16 and 17th resulted in the decision to temporarily base major units of the Home Fleet on Scottish West coast anchorages, a fair cruising distance from their operating areas in the North Sea and North Eastern Atlantic Ocean.

On 17 October, the day Scapa Flow was bombed, eight mobile 3.7 in guns had been moved to Rosyth as a first move in planning that called for the provision of a 72 gun system for the defence of the base/docs and anchorages.[100] The plan that called for the more than doubling of the available anti-aircraft defences at Rosyth also included the allocation of searchlights, close-range anti-aircraft 'pom pom' guns, a balloon barrage and additional fighter aircraft squadrons.[101] This, it was hoped, would make Rosyth a secure main anchorage for the Home Fleet pending its return to Scapa Flow. However, the Chief of the Air Staff noted that 'No matter how many fighters, guns and other defences we might place at Rosyth, the German Air Force, if prepared to launch a really heavy scale of attack against the Fleet at anchor there, would inevitably inflict some damage'.[102] This fact was recognised by the First Lord of the Admiralty, contributing to the decision to move the Home Fleet to the relative safety of the West coast of Scotland, temporarily.

In regards to Rosyth, among the most visible near term air defence improvements was the installation of No.992 Squadron Balloon Barrage, which was moved from the defenses of the City of Glasgow. The fighter defences in Scotland were increased, including the deployment of three Hawker Hurricane

---

[98] W.P. 39(94) Weekly Resume No.7, 12 Noon, 12th October to 12 Noon, 19th October, 1939

[99] It should be noted that some additional defence measures were already in the works in relation to providing increased security at the Royal Navies main anchorages

[100] W.M. (39) 51st Conclusions, Minute 4. Confidential Annex. H.M.S. Royal Oak, Security of Fleet Bases. Richmond Terrance, S.W.1, 18th October, 1939. See also C.O.S. (39) 51st Meeting, War Cabinet, Chiefs of Staff Committee, Minutes of Meeting held on 18th October, 1939, at 10..45 a.m.

[101] W.M. (39) 52nd Conclusions, Minute 5. Confidential Annex. Security of Fleet Bases. Defence of Rosyth. Richmond Terrance, S.W.1, 19th October, 1939. The pom pom was a quick firing 2 pounder/40 mm calibre weapon, typically a four barrel mount

[102] W.M. (39) 52nd Conclusions, Minute 5. Confidential Annex. Security of Fleet Bases, Defence of Rosyth. This document details the provision of Fighter defences would have been as follows: 'Two squadrons would be stationed at Rosyth permanently; a third would be added when there was a capital ship in dry-dock, and a total of four squadrons would be there when the whole Fleet was present'

monoplane fighter Squadrons to Wick in the very North of the Scottish mainland to cover Scapa Flow, which also had the first elements of a Balloon Barrage from No.950 Squadron in operation by March 1940.[103] It was that month that, with the improved air defences and improved protection from submarine attack, the Home Fleet moved from the Scottish West coast anchorages back to Scapa Flow, elements continuing to be based on Rosyth in the Firth of Forth, which was now considerably better protected against air attack than had hitherto been the case.

It is clear that when the effects of the decision to base ships on Scottish west coast anchorages, a not inconsiderable distance from their operating areas in the North Sea and Eastern Atlantic Ocean, is considered, then the German losses sustained in the air attacks - four aircraft - can be considered light.[104] The German actions had forced a change in British defensive policy to the effect that Royal Navy warships, in particular capital ships and cruisers, were now less readily available for operations where they were needed – to counter any potential German invasion force, however unlikely invasion seemed in 1939. Such ships were also less readily disposed to deal with German surface raiders attempting to break out into the North Atlantic Ocean, a situation of extreme importance for a nation dependent on sea trade for her very survival. While the media of the time, and some prominent military/political figures, tried to downplay the effects of the German air raids as a pitiful waste of three aircraft for no commensurable return, others were more reserved in their assessments.[105] Post war, when public moral was not a factor, those more reserved assessments could be heard. Of the movement of the Home Fleet to the Clyde on the west coast of Scotland it was remarked, 'Thence it would be difficult, to say the least, for our ships to intercept with due speed a surface-raider breaking into the Atlantic or a force descending on our east coast. By two or three boldly directed strokes, and a total cost of four aircraft [this apparently takes into account the Ju.88 that crashed in Holland on its return from the 16 October air raid], the German Air Force and U-boat Service had between them scored a resounding strategic success – of which, very fortunately, the German Navy was to take little advantage'.[106]

---

[103] Wick lies on the North East coast of the Scottish mainland some 30 km or so from Scapa Flow

[104] The German aircraft losses included two shot down during the attack on the Firth of Forth on 16 October 1939 and one shot down during the attack on Scapa Flow the following day. Unknown to the British High Command at the time, a fourth German bomber, succumbing to damage inflicted during the air raid on 16 October 1939, had crashed in Holland on its return, all four crew perishing

[105] Four German aircraft were lost when the Ju.88 that crashed in Holland on its return from rain on the Forth is taken into account

The available evidence clearly shows that the raid, far from being arbitrary, was part of a coordinated German campaign against the Home Fleet at anchor or underway in British coastal waters. The losses on the British side were heavier than those suffered by the German side, although neither were severe in that it did not significantly affect the respective forces operational capability. The resultant move of the Home Fleet to Scottish West coast anchorages was undoubtedly the most serious effect of the submarine and air raids of the 14th, 16th and 15th of October 1939, this causing a shortfall in operational capability for the Home Fleet until the issue of strengthening of the defences of the Firth of Forth and Scapa Flow was sufficiently advanced to redress the situation that had existed in October 1939.

[106] Richards, *The Royal Air Force 1939-1945, Vol. I*, 67

ADDENDUM I

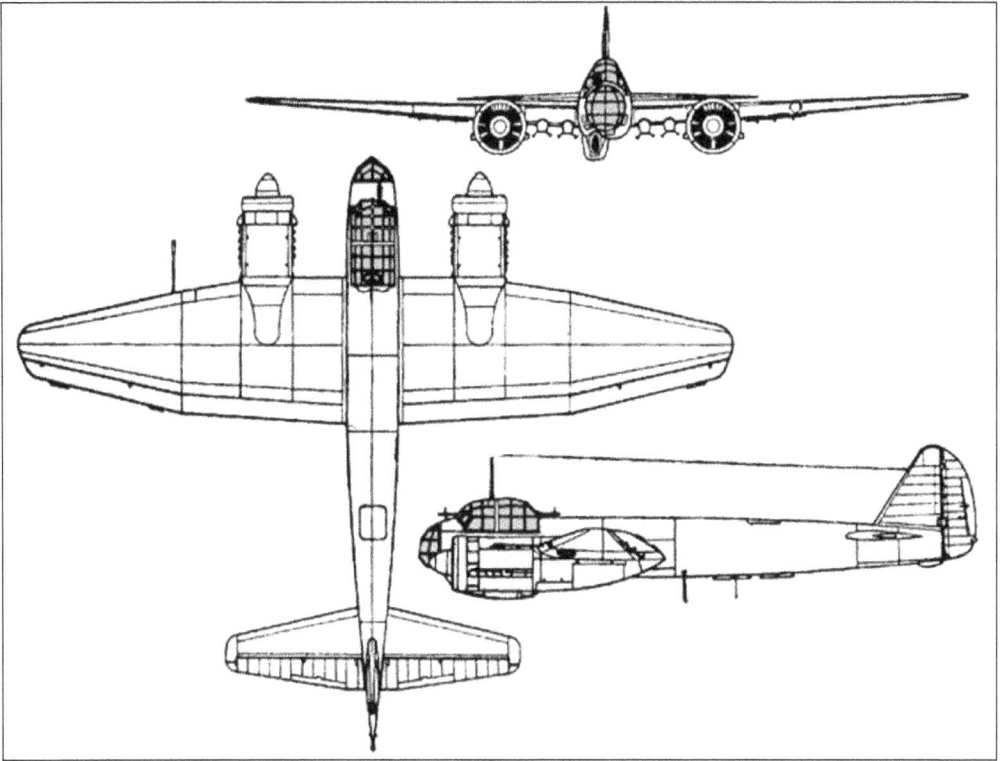

Figure 10. Ju.88A of a similar model to those employed against warships in the Forth Estuary on 16 October 1939. The Junkers 88 was a modern (for the time) twin-engine monoplane medium bomber aircraft with a crew of four. As well as the offensive armament of bombs the aircraft carried forward and rearward firing defensive machine guns for protection against enemy fighter aircraft. The Ju.88A had a maximum speed in the order of 285 mph, this being attained at an altitude of around 16,000 ft. This maximum speed of some 70 mph less than the Spitfire MK I monoplane fighter aircraft allowed the latter to intercept the German bombers and conduct multiple firing passes.

Figure 11. A Ju.88 circa 1940.

Figure 12. Ju.88 of an undetermined unit in summer 1940. CC

Figure 13. This flight formation of Ju.88's employed over France, the Low Countries and Britain in summer 1940, arguably afforded better protection from fighter attack, but was more highly conspicuous and better suited to level bombing. It was therefore, not adopted by *I/Kampfgeschwader 30* for the attack on 16 October 1939. CC

ADDENDUM II

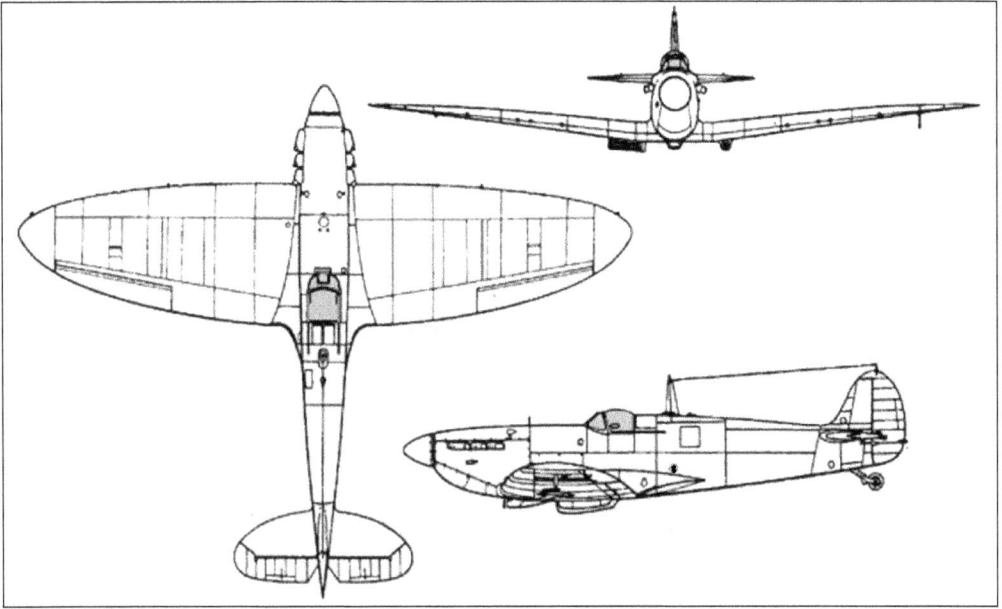

Figure 14. Supermarine Spitfire MK.I monoplane fighter.CC

Figure 15. The Spitfire MK I was a single seat monoplane fighter aircraft with a maximum level speed of around 355 mph at an altitude of around 19,000 ft. The aircraft armament consisted of eight wing mounted 0.303 inch Browning machine guns – four housed in each wing. Its high speed allowed the aircraft to intercept the Ju.88 bombers and conduct multiple firing passes. This aircraft above, which served with 19 Squadron in summer 1940, is representative of the Spitfire MK.I that served with 602 and 603 Squadrons in October 1939. CC

Figure 16. The Spitfire MK.I had entered RAF service in 1938. This publicity photograph shows of a quintet of early examples fitted with twin blade propellers in 1938. CC

ADDENDUM III

Figure 17. The Light Cruiser HMS *Edinburgh* of the Edinburgh Class in the Mediterranean in August 1941 whilst employed on Malta convoy escort duties. CC

HMS *Edinburgh*
Displacement: 10,000 tons.
Length: 613.5 ft. overall
Beam: 63 ft.
Draft (draught): 17.25 ft.
Speed: 32.5 knots
Guns: 12 x 6 inch, 12 x 4 in AA, 4 x 3 pounder and 16 x smaller calibre weapons
Torpedo tubes: 6 x 21 inch (tripled)
Aircraft: 4, launched from a single catapult launch system

Table 1. Basic characteristics of HMS *Edinburgh* of the Edinburgh Class Light Cruiser.[107]

---

[107] FM-30-51, War Department Basic Filed Manual, Military Intelligence, Identification of British Naval Ships, December 29, 1941 (United States Government Printing Office, Washington, 1942). Note. The basic characteristics provided correspond to 1941 and may differ slightly in some respects, such as the smaller calibre armament and perhaps displacement, to that of 1939

Figure 18. HMS *Edinburgh* underway near Scapa Flow in October 1941. CC

Figure 19. HMS *Edinburgh* cruising in the vicinity of Scapa Flow in 1941. CC

Figure 20. Light Cruiser of the Southampton Class. HMS *Southampton* was lost on 11.01.1941 due to uncontrollable fires as a result of several direct hits with 500 lb. class bombs while the cruiser was escorting a convoy in the Mediterranean Sea. CC

HMS *Southampton*

Displacement: 9,100 tons.
Length: 591.5 ft. overall
Beam: 61 and two thirds ft.
Draft: 17 ft. mean
Speed: 32 knots
Guns: 12 x 6 inch, 8 x 4 in AA, 1 x 3.7 howitzer, 4 x 3 pounder and 16 x smaller calibre weapons
Torpedo tubes: 6 x 21 inch (tripled)
Aircraft: 3, launched from a single catapult launch system

Table 2. Basic characteristics of HMS *Southampton* of the Southampton Class Light Cruiser.[108]

---

[108] FM-30-51, War Department Basic Filed Manual, Military Intelligence, Identification of British Naval Ships, December 29, 1941 (United States Government Printing Office, Washington, 1942). Note. The basic characteristics provided correspond to 1941 and may differ slightly in some respects, such as the smaller calibre armament and perhaps displacement, to that of 1939

Figure 20. Tribal Class Destroyer HMS *Mohawk*.

HMS *Mohawk*

Displacement: 1,870 tons.
Length: 355.5 ft. overall
Beam: 36.5 ft.
Draft: 9 ft. mean
Speed: 36.5 knots
Guns: 8 x 4.7 inch, and seven smaller caliber weapons
Torpedo tubes: 4 x 21 inch

Table 3. Basic characteristics of the Tribal Class Destroyer HMS *Mohawk*.[109]

---

[109] FM-30-51, War Department Basic Filed Manual, Military Intelligence, Identification of British Naval Ships, December 29, 1941 (United States Government Printing Office, Washington, 1942). Note. The basic characteristics provided correspond to 1941 and may differ slightly in some respects, such as the smaller calibre armament and perhaps displacement, to that of 1939

BIBLIOGRAPHY

Richards, Denis. *History of the Second Word War, The Royal Air Force 1939-1945, Vol. I: The Fight At Odds*, United Kingdom Military Series, London, HMSO, 1953

Collier, Basil. *History of the Second World War, The Defence of the United Kingdom*, United Kingdom Military Series, London, HMSO, 1957

Roskill, S.W. *History of the Second World War, The War at Sea 1939-1945, Volume I: The Defensive*, United Kingdom Military Series, London, HMSO, 1954

No.602 City of Glasgow (Bombing) (Fighter) Squadron, Auxiliary Air Force, Form 540, Summary of Events, for January 1939

No.602 City of Glasgow (Fighter) Squadron, Auxiliary Air Force, Form 540, Summary of Events, for May 1939

No.602 City of Glasgow (Fighter) Squadron, Auxiliary Air Force, Form 540, Summary of Events, for September 1939

No.602 City of Glasgow (Fighter) Squadron, Auxiliary Air Force, Form 540, Summary of Events, for October 1939

No.602 Squadron Form 540, Detail of Work Carried Out, 16 October 1939
No.603 Squadron, Form 541, Record of Events, Detail of Work Carried Out from 1430. hrs. 16/10/39 to 1630 hrs. 16/10/39

No.603 Squadron, Summary of Events, Form 540 for October 1939

No.603 Squadron Form 541, Detail of Work Carried Out, from 1435 hrs. 22/10/39 to 1525 hrs., 22/10/39

AIR/50/167 No.603 Squadron Form F Combat Report, 16.10.1939 (F/Lt. Gifford, F/O. Macdonald and P/O. Robertson)

AIR/50/166 No.602 Squadron Form F Combat Report 16.10.1939

W.P. 39(94). (Also paper No. C.O.S. (39)92). War Cabinet. Weekly Resume No.7 of the Naval, Military and Air Situation (12 Noon, 12th October to 12 Noon, 19th October, 1939)

W.P. (39)101. (Also paper No. C.O.S. (39)103). War Cabinet. Weekly Resume No.8 of the Naval, Military and Air Situation (12 Noon, 19th October to 12 Noon, 26th October, 1939)

The War Office, The Anti-Aircraft Defence of the United Kingdom, From 28 July 1939, to 15 April 1945, Supplement to the London Gazette, 1947

Survey of the A.A. Defence of the United Kingdom, Vol. II

War Cabinet (39) 50th, Conclusions of a Meeting of the War Cabinet held at 10 Downing Street, S.W., on Tuesday, October 17, 1939, at 11.30 A.M.

War Cabinet (39) 51, Conclusions of a Meeting of the War Cabinet held at 10 Downing Street, S.W., on Wednesday, October 18, 1939, at 11.30 A.M.

War Cabinet (39) 52, Conclusions of a Meeting of the War Cabinet held at 10 Downing Street, S.W., on Thursday, October 19, 1939, at 11.30 A.M.

W.M. (39) 49th Conclusions, Minute 3. Confidential Annex., Naval Situation. Richmond Terrance, S.W.1, 16th October, 1939

W.M. (39) 51st Conclusions, Minute 4. Confidential Annex., H.M.S. Royal Oak, Security of Fleet Bases. Richmond Terrance, S.W.1, 18th October, 1939

W.M. (39) 52nd Conclusions, Minute 5. Confidential Annex., Security of Fleet Bases. Defence of Rosyth. Richmond Terrance, S.W.1, 19th October, 1939

B.R.186(2) ([initially C.B. 4273 (52)] H.M. Ships Damaged or Sunk by Enemy Action, 3rd Sept. 1939 to 2nd Sept. 1945 (1952)

GB 1212b, Queensferry (Firth of Forth) from German intelligence report

C.O.S. (39) 50th Meeting, War Cabinet, Chiefs of Staff Committee, Minutes of Meeting held on 17th October, 1939, at 10..45 a.m.

C.O.S. (39) 51st Meeting, War Cabinet, Chiefs of Staff Committee, Minutes of Meeting held on 18th October, 1939, at 10..45 a.m.

C.O.S. (39) 57th Meeting, War Cabinet, Chiefs of Staff Committee, Minutes of Meeting held on 24th October, 1939, at 10..45 a.m.

C.O.S. (39) 52nd Meeting, War Cabinet, Chiefs of Staff Committee, Minutes of Meeting held on 19th October, 1939, at 10..45 a.m.

War Cabinet Paper No. C.O.8. (39)103

A.M. Pamphlet (Monograph) No.248

A.M., A.H.B.-6 (Files of the Quartermaster General, German Air Ministry)

FM-30-51, War Department Basic Filed Manual, Military Intelligence, Identification of British Naval Ships, December 29, 1941, United States Government Printing Office Washington, 1942

Harkins, Hugh, Unpublished Research paper on Spitfire I/II performance comparison

GLOSSARY

AA	Anti-Aircraft
CC	Crown Copyright
COS	Chiefs of Staff
F/Lt.	Flight Lieutenant
F/O	Flying Officer
ft.	Feet (unit of measurement)
HA	High Angle
HMS	His Majesty's Ship
HMSO	Her Majesty's Stationary Office
I	Roman numeral number I
II	Roman numeral number II
III	Roman numeral number III
Ju	Junkers
km	Kilometers
mph	Miles per hour
No.	Number
P/O	Pilot Officer
RAF	Royal Air Force
RDF	Radio Direction Finding
U	Undersea

ABOUT THE AUTHOR

Hugh Harkins, FRAS is a historian and author with an extensive background in astro/geophysics and studies/research in the wider scientific, aeronautic, astronautic and nautical technical and historical fields. Hugh has published in excess of sixty books; non-fiction and fiction, writing under his given name as well as utilising several pseudonyms. He has also written for several international magazines, whilst his work has been used as reference for many other projects ranging from the aviation industry, international news corporations and film media to encyclopaedias, museum exhibits and the computer gaming industry. Hugh is a member of the Institute of Physics and is an elected Fellow of the Royal Astronomical Society. He currently resides in his native Scotland. Other titles by the author include:

Iskander - Mobile Tactical Aero-Ballistic/Cruise Missile Complex
Orbital/Fractional Orbit Bombardment System - The Soviet Globalnaya Raketa
Counter-Space Defence Co-Orbital Satellite Fighter
Sukhoi T-50/PAK FA - Russia's 5th Generation 'Stealth' Fighter
Sukhoi Su-35S 'Flanker' E - Russia's 4++ Generation Super-Manoeuvrability Fighter
Sukhoi Su-34 'Fullback'
Sukhoi Su-30MKK/MK2/M2 - Russo Kitashiy Striker from Amur
MiG-35/D 'Fulcrum' F – Towards the Fifth Generation
Air War over Syria, Tu-160, Tu-95MS & Tu-22M3 - Cruise Missile and Bombing Strikes on Syria, November 2015-February 2016
Sukhoi Su-27SM(3)/SKM
Russian/Soviet Aircraft Carrier & Carrier Aviation Design & Evolution Volume 1 - Seaplane Carriers, Project 71/72, Graf Zeppelin, Project 1123 ASW Cruiser & Project 1143-1143.4 Heavy Aircraft Carrying Cruiser
Light Battle Cruisers and the Second Battle of Heligoland Bight
British Battlecruisers of World War 1 - Operational Log, July 1914-June 1915
Eurofighter Typhoon - Storm over Europe
Tornado F.2/F.3 Air Defence Variant
Air to Air Missile Directory
North American F-108 Rapier - Mach 3 Interceptor
Convair YB-60 - Fort Worth Overcast
Boeing X-36 Tailless Agility Flight Research Aircraft
X-32 - The Boeing Joint Strike Fighter
X-35 - Progenitor to the F-35 Lightning II
X-45 Uninhabited Combat Air Vehicle
Into The Cauldron - The Lancaster MK.I Daylight Raid on Augsburg
Hurricane IIB Combat Log - 151 Wing RAF, North Russia 1941
RAF Meteor Jet Fighters in World War II, an Operational Log
Typhoon IA/B Combat Log - Operation Jubilee, August 1942
Defiant MK.I Combat Log - Fighter Command, May-September 1940
Blenheim MK.IF Combat Log - Fighter Command Day Fighter Sweeps/Night Interceptions, September 1939 - June 1940
Tomahawk I/II Combat Log - European Theatre, 1941-42
Fortress MK.I Combat Log - Bomber Command High Altitude Bombing Operations, July-September 1941
XF-92 - Convairs Arrow

www.ingramcontent.com/pod-product-compliance
Lightning Source LLC
Chambersburg PA
CBHW081242020426
42331CB00013B/3264